Thundering on the Pink

Thundering on the Pink

Poems by

Trisha Leigh Shufelt

Cover design by Shay Culligan
Cover image originally by Jon Tyson on Unsplash,
printed with colors adjusted
Author photo by Trisha Leigh Shufelt

ISBN: 979-8-90146-728-2
Library of Congress Control Number: 2026935933

Kelsay Books
502 South 1040 East, A-119
American Fork, Utah 84003
Kelsaybooks.com

Other Books by the Author

Trisha's Books

Liminal Lines—Poetry & prose

Liminal Lessons—Poetry & prose

Break & Bloom—Poetry & prose

The Ghosts of Nevermore—Poetry, prose, & short stories inspired by the works of Edgar Allan Poe. Received the 2023 Saturday Visiter Award, Poe House & Museum of Baltimore, MD

The Ghosts of Winterbourne—Poetry & prose

Sunder the Silence—Poetry & prose

Unearthing Nevermore—Golden shovel poetry inspired by Edgar Allan Poe

Avenoir—Poetry & prose

Penning Paper Moths—Poetry

The Underwood Wicked Fairytale Series—Novels published under the name Andaleigh Archer

Anthologies

Raven's Quoth Press: *Evermore 2 & 4*

300 South Street Publishing: *Love is Helpless; Immortal Tales; Shadow of the Soul; Quail Bell Magazine; & Heretics, Lovers, and Madmen*

Keeping the Flame Alive Press: *Keeping the Flame Alive Issue 11*

Self-Transformation Works

The Poe Tarot (Schiffer Publishing/RedFeatherMBS)—Nominated for a 2022 Saturday Visiter Award through the Poe House & Museum of Baltimore, MD. Winner of a Bronze 2022 COVR Visionary Award

The Everglow Divination System (Schiffer Publishing/RedFeather-MBS)

Contents

PART TWO

For Andy

PART ONE

Poets
bleed words
from hidden thorns
inside a book of roses
read.

Thoughts on a Napkin

I see her, yellow flower
behind chipped milky glass
sipping stagnant neglect
neck bent sideways, broken

lungs full of dirty secrets
begging to release
thick torment of truths
choking sticky exhale

if only she could
wipe her thoughts clean
instead of dropping dead petals
on a stained café napkin.

Hymns of Never Again

Turn the knob
back to piney branches
to shiny green bicycle
and vivid orange shag carpet

to fingers mothing
whisker shafts of wheat
coxing memory
in each feather brush

it's twilight
another day—lost
wishful possibility—
gone

another day
disavows vows by hours
unripened prayers fold
into neat envelopes

tithings to scars
ringing like broken bells
as ministers scream hymns
do you hear me?

silence the child
let the last lemon of sun
retreat without litany
let its holy ghost die

behind brown needles
let green rust to orange
erode metal wounds
let rain salt you clean

release cradled cries
let *amens* halo darkling skies
pearl thorns into crowns and sing
latent hymns of *Never Again.*

House of Fog

At the end of the world
sits a house of fog
where walls are unsent letters

each crack and crevice
finds me cerebral
forever searching for light

like a trapped moth
whose escape is hidden
on a pinhead of dust

the house is a creature
shedding skin
in peeling wallpaper flowers

its heart creaks
in illusion's disbelief
its voice is a whistle

from a broken window
calling for a child
it birthed long ago.

Snail

I was seven
you insisted I watch you
pour salt on its tiny body

watch as it shrank
smaller than its shell
but all I saw was your face

the malice behind your eyes
knowing death was unfair
death could come at any time

and I knew you killed it
not because we had a garden
not because we were overrun

you killed it for pleasure
it was smaller
and I was smaller

and you were a giant
crushing and killing
us both for fun.

Thundering on the Pink

The night smells
rusty and raw
like a potato birthed
inside damp Earthen womb

coating me copper and sticky
making my brain into a circus tent
overrun with stomping elephants
thundering on the pink

a nebula of cotton candy
weaving a childhood carousel
no longer pastel colored and sweet
it screeches metal on metal, *eat me*

I oblige, starving for iron
and spit stones, I toss at mirrors
reflecting a river of buried ghosts
surfacing with truthful epiphanies

damn your poetry, she says
draining the dredge beneath,
and I think, good,
I am empty now

I am what she wanted
hollow and transparent
abstract and ambiguous
like a slow, dissipating fog.

Dream Therapy

I'm trapped inside
the disorder of a dream
eating cake covered walls
on a bramble-baked brownstone

my teeth are daggers
cutting through the once was
coring secret never seeds
from an overripe mind

I'm tossing thoughts
like rotten apples
into a compost heap
of shattered bird bones

oh, woeful night
they are my fallen muses
no longer green feathered
but silent charred corpses

blacked, bloodless leaves
between aging thighs
sharp-edged and splintered
shriveled in broken regret

their once wet aches
now dry mouthed
and plumbed of spirit
die with eyes wide open.

Rabbits on a Roundabout

I was walking
alone in a park
near an elementary school
when I spotted two rabbits

they've been scarce to find
but I saw them today
one as small as a chipmunk
timid tale and tiny ears

peeking above a patch
of white Spring clover
mama in the hedges
a few feet away

it reminded me
of walking to and from school
before the morning sun
reached awakening sky

8-year-old me
avoiding sylvan shortcuts
behind our apartment
for a *safe* concrete path

rope and keys around my neck
latchkey kids, they called us—
home alone kids
because both parents worked

Mom told me
walk with friends
but I didn't have any
so, I walked alone

my fidgety white fingertips
inside hand-me-down mittens
lead weight frozen toes cramping
inside Buster Brown shoes

blood pooling welts on my legs
neith Oshkosh B'Gosh jeans
hiding the words I'd written
on my skin with a fingernail

I feared I would be taken
like little Adam Walsh
be the next face on a milk carton
stranger danger, lost

we just had reminders
don't take candy from strangers
but what about the candy
from those we knew

we were no longer safe
but didn't know it, yet
and our parents couldn't see it
the insidious evolution

they had their own baggage
they had their own weight
their parent's choices and
the wars that came before

most were Silent, some Boomed
living behind unlocked doors
traditionalism to individualism
seen and not heard, to loud and proud

we were Gen X
the unknown variables
the MTV generation
with free-range parents

It's 10 p.m.,
do you know where your children are?

starting dinner for ourselves
cleaning and doing laundry
absorbing a vicious cycle
of imprints on wash, rinse, repeat

we were Kramer vs. Kramer kids
cynical and sundered
we were the outside children
the last of the feral, wild

living through bare feet
mud-covered and sweaty
always on the brink
of nuclear annihilation

40-year-olds, trapped
inside 10-year-old bodies
we fell a thousand times
into our own arms

suppressed
and pressed down
decompressed inward
unheard and unseen

until we became rabbits
still wild inside, still muddy
imprinting our litter, watching
always watching above the clover.

Acorns in the Sacrosanct Woods

I imagine writing poems
the way acorns dream
of the trees they might become—
beautiful and everlasting

still, imprints heat internal ink
impulses retreat into dying bloom
anticipating the Never
they might never become

sputtering and stuttering
words within worlds
writ upon the dying leaf
fearful of falling

failing leaves of paper
hitting the ground, screaming
bland and colorless
as falling Snow

a noiseless blanket
threaded with ice
unheard words mutilating
neith bloodless briars

oh, would these thoughts become cypselae—
release and fly into dandelion wishes
or prayers of hopeful seeds
no longer weeds of blasphemy.

Library

There's a Virgoan order
to your library of extractions
neatly categorized and
labeled for another day

files of youthful mistakes
peer reviewed journals
microfiches of the past
all foxing poetically

things you wished you'd said
backlogs of rehearsed scripts
for the next argument or
heartbreak ending

still bristling with bruises
and hindsight epiphanies
last but not least
sealed inside attic archives

are cautious reminders
in case of emergency
whose shelf is titled
the banned—

people, places, and things
echoing shadows
one should never revisit
and remain buried.

Time Is a Drunk Poet

You remain frozen
in Time's memory
where you do not age
until you do

and I am shocked awake
present in Time's palm
who eats without regret
insatiable and cruel

in Time's gluttony
what does it leave behind
while everything else
goes on forever

while everything else
lives free of its appetite
until it doesn't
and I am

grasping at straws
wondering when
it will be my time or
wondering when, or if Time

will draw the shortest straw
drink in what I see spilling
from a drunk poet's cup
and choke on the contents.

Looking Through a Window

I am a window
outside of myself
looking inward
through a screen

the night rushes
with its shadows
gathering moths
toward false light

winging my brain
their hindsight flutters
against scarred memories
alive without allegory

I am meaningful
aware of purpose
as though all secrets
pass through me

in a sneeze
I am bright
starlit from within
a shining full moon

aglow with magic
fully blossoming
wholeness illuminated
despite a broken frame.

An Observation at a Local Café

Two pawns
sit across from each other
engaged in a chess match
contemplating next moves

each believing
they hold checkmate
I imagine they are apple peels
curling away from sweetness

naked in yellow fiction
revealing cored secrets
behind sips of loathing

exhaustion underlies smoky exhales
rising with steam
from tea-stained cups
filled with uncomfortable silences

it's a better story, isn't it
pretending people are poems
peeling apart layers, hidden
behind grieving hours

each winning games
despite stinging glances
and stale distance mothing
inside regretful mouths.

The Collective River

The world feels grape skin thin
rotting from the inside out
like tossed fruit boats
stagnating a lazy river

is it easier to backstroke
on a current of chaos
is it easier to hold your breath
under the water of toxic ignorance

is it easier to buoy on backs
of the drowning without realizing
you are the bloating dredge—
polluting the collective wake.

Used Shoes

I love a used pair of shoes
worn in and comfortable
days of walking places
I've never seen

today, I'm wearing brown leather
Mary Jane's from New Orleans
scuff marks on the heels
and a bit more on the toes

endless strolls, I imagine
through the French Quarter
on sticky summer nights or
visits to Marie Laveau's grave

I can feel their energy
blackened soles, curling inward
like the previous owner's toes
gripping haunted ground

maybe she stopped for a rest
at Café du Monde in the morning
had a coffee and a beignet
or danced behind a jazz funeral

oh, the place you’ve seen
what a fantastical life
these shoes have led
before finding my humble feet.

Letters to Your Scars

I've hidden secrets
in skin pockets
envelopes of scars
childhood to now

fostered in cell memory
witnessed, helpless, and battle weary
the unsaid and said, buried deep
inside loss-mingled happiness

times I wished for ignorance
times I prayed for death
clung to bits of hope, floating
cradling me to unknown destinations

I've been reluctant to surrender
my imprints and fears
threaded with lies
unjustified

anxiety-laced years
lost and drowning in merlot
smiling through tears
masking the pain

specifically, there are questions
wonder whys
begging for answers
but I've heard

we choose these paths
have already chosen them—
contracts of reckoning
a deal before the dawn

and if that is true
resistance is futile
everything is the right path
to what we already know

so, gather the scraps
of endless poetry
pitted with pith
wedged in sour

save the ink for rainy days
when latent hunger
begs for a morsel
or moral to a story

drafts of blood
you've yet to write
filling in miles of nothingness
anticipating miles of something more.

Oz

We were the last
feral children
living like Monarchs
in imaginary kingdoms

viridescent color
flying toward sunlight
our unseen butterfly wings
shadowing Poplar snow

we were foxes
in red bliss freedom
pained only by the flickering
street lamp call to go home

removing our costumes
and layers of embalmed earth
with hosed-down baths
and prayer bargains before bed

we were barefoot
and brave, picking bottle glass
from black, callused heels
pretending everything was magic

that captured firefly
that stick sword
that mudpie
those fake cigarettes

it didn’t matter
because everything mattered
and life—
it was ours.

Kiss and Tell

I got my first kiss
when I was eleven
a blond-haired, blue-eyed farm boy
named Timmy

sitting in the back of a church bus
headed to Sunday school
I thought for sure
we'd go to Hell

my second kiss
was a French kiss
from a guy named Cliff
I was sixteen

he was high as a kite
shoved his weedy tongue
in my mouth without invitation
I thought I was in Hell

my third kiss
was my first love
he kissed another
I hoped he'd burn in hell

my fourth kiss
made me realize
Hell wasn’t a place
Hell was a choice

my fifth kiss burned
like the fires of Hell
and I knew with everything holy
Heaven was real.

Bonfire Eulogy

When I die
burn me bright
include my books
everything said or unsaid

let everything flame
into a great bonfire
let me ink smoky poetry
on the sky's blue parchment

grieve or rejoice
then wash me away
and any remaining embers
with rhyme and rain.

Slow Spring

Oh, give me her slow Spring
give me endless walks
'neath cerulean brushed skies

thaw my aching bones
ignite my tired eyes
to amber, woodland wonder

give me perfumed yellow bouquets
green shoots commingling
raw leaf decay turning

breath of Earthly yawn shaking
Winter slumber awakening
inside her damp restless womb.

That's All

There are days
I pretend I am Plath
days, I know I am
channel crossing her spirit

spinning on spider legs
with a lampshade brain
full of poetry and
disquieting muses

sucking on nothing but madness
and plums of purple prose
borrowed and baked
in a broken *Easy Bake Oven*

days I play dress up
despite my wizened stem
don a red wig
and eat my man like air

days where I am
unsure if I am or wishing I was
more than the I am
I have become.

My Life in Pictures

I realize as the hours wane
I have not truly lived
but spent a lifetime dying

wondering what ifs
behind safety glass
and now, feeling pathetic

nostalgia and regrets
line every inch of crepey skin
aching my bloodless bones—

while fear keeps me from flying,
and Paris will always be a picture
hanging on my wall.

Onward

chafing noise
teeth-clinching static
bracing breath
on imbalanced feet

tangling backward
into hazy retreat
wrecking the night
of peaceful sleep

choking words
with sorrows deep
until the din thins
Memory's keep

where awakening begins
before imprints
forked tongue and
bound your brain

in chained anchors
of discordant refrain
imbalanced harmony
beside tainted words

writ in bitterness
on Skin's book
of lined remembrance
onward until stillness

hangs a single note
resolution resounds
wreckage afloat
listen and remember

dissonance running deep
remember, *it weeps*
red notes from
a bleeding book.

But First, Coffee

I miss staying up late
sleeping in like a rockstar
something I haven't done
since age twenty-five

now, my body clock wakes me
dawning demands shake me
feed the cat her crunchies
the to-do list is waiting

chop, chop,
the day is slipping away
no time to play
Alice is grown now

I miss when time stood still
and thirty seemed far away
didn't worry about aging parents
or my shrinking 401k

when a hot flash
was random gossip
and what to have for dinner
didn't feel like a chore

a Flintstones Vitamin
got me through the day
now, each passing year
has me closer to Death's door

but then I remember
fresh-brewed coffee
and books I've yet to read
simple pleasures are all I need

I also remember
I still have poetry left to write
some hidden in my attic mind
and much in visible sight

like falling in love with the ordinary
is extraordinarily affined to peace,
and important lessons are learned
when we endeavor to release

I didn't know this at twenty
but now at fifty-five
it's me first, then the cat
everything else, the coffee decides.

Threshold

How many times have you stood
on the precipice of possibility
only to turn away
forgo an unknown future
for familiar comfort
was it fear of failure
forcing your feet to flee

oh, my friend
look to the sky
the bird does not blanch
the blue beyond
she trusts her wings
knowing the wait
will wither wishes and
keep her from the worm.

PART TWO

Petals
Bleed color
From hidden thorns
Neith sugar water crystal
Façade

Confessional

I pour a glass
of your favorite color
drink it like a Judas kiss
full of sin and contrition

ginger waves
coat my confessions
hidden behind closed cloisters
in a stained-glass church
of liquid tithe.

Mr. Darcy was a Poet

Mr. Darcy read his poetry from behind a silver mike stand. Trading his navy tailcoat for a weatherworn bomber, he looked like a rockstar under the heather of the English Pub's false gel lights. His inky-black hair feathering his face gave him the appearance of an unholy raven longing for the Eyrie of his home.

And when he spoke, autumn berries kissed his parted lips, igniting fire to the myth of his whisky sonnet. His forest eyes, full of ghosts, peeled me naked like summer birch. And I sighed against the lacy, wet pulse of everything I desired and feared, falling under the spell he'd cast, bewitching me body and soul.

A Prayer to the Pocket Stone

Say, you are not a passing thing
a figment of my imagination
mothing toward false light

say, you are a seed
born from a pocket stone
smoothed between fitful fingers

a myth manifested in my mythos
dreamed from a whispered prayer
of infinite future yesterdays

say, I read about you
birthed you in a cosmic tome
from my childhood library

or spun you like wool
dyed from Poet's ink
threading an ancient loom
laced with lost melancholy

however, you came to be
no matter the thimble of time
we have left to share

sew the seasons with me
until the trees grow tired
of begging leaves to bleed
their need for color.

Poetry of the Day

You cling to me
skin warm with sleep
kiss me like Keats
dance me again

on a floor mattress
of crumpled linen flowers
I fall into your poetry
blocking Day's demands

desire dives deep
into every part of you
where love isn't a full stop but
a place where I burn like the sun.

Orchard

While the world slept
we were a haunted orchard
bathing in hidden colors
you, naked with smile

fawn eyes dancing
drunk on burgundy wine
your lips, honey, sweet
like Mission Figs

unlike me, bruised grape
clinging to weighted branches
longing to feel
fearing to fall

into the velvet night
ripe and split open
like an orchard plum
glistening in the dark.

One Word

If this is the final hour
if I am alone in my restless bower
and all that was, is, and shall ever be
retreats to nothingness

I will surrender to endless sleep
I will succumb without hesitation
into a coffin of inky mesmerization
but *I will* beg for one memory

to ease the unknown journey
one sound echoing eternity
one word in its holy poetry
spun from scraps of sky

one, others mocked and denied
yet you, married to memories
of starlight and naked dawn
colored with sea and birdsong

hope and promising tomorrows
awakening the wild with wonder
from quiet sighs and fervent love
echoing like thunder

one word
one sliver
one sound
a dulcet whisper

leading but never leaving
beyond needle
of Death's lonely door—
my name on your breath, forevermore.

Fireflies in a Jar

We held too much of us
in the palm of our hands
radiating sun, burning
centers of universe

infusing dreams
with cider light
we were fireflies
inside a jar

captured illumination
of carousel thoughts tripping
inside a Van Gogh painting
we were secrets swirling

behind stained-glass eyes
aching for amens in poetry
brush stroking each other
in kissing prayers

unraveling disparate forevers
written from velvet ache
of who we thought we were
and who we longed to be

begging swarms of bees
not to sting
our honeyed dive
for divinity.

Rooms on Fire

I sometimes wonder
what would have happened if
you had walked away that night
when I told you to let me go

where would we be
would you still be there
shrinking into nothingness
or find a different escape

would I stop looking for you
in the eyes of every stranger
or seeking you
in the touch of every lover

would we know true love
if this love was the one
we let slip away
would our hearts heal

would time make us forget
the faces we once wore
the names we endured
grieve away or blur the edges

I’m glad we didn’t listen
to anyone who said
we were wrong
or to ourselves

when we said
we were wrong—
it’s impossible to deny
a destination of Souls

we would have found a way
in this lifetime or the next
still, we chose this one,
and I love who we became

thirty years on
in the blink of an eye
gone are the loud nights
with their strobes of color

gone are the late mornings
spent in beds of thunder
the bad habits we once fed
fears of the unknowns ahead

thirty years still holding hands
when we drift off to sleep
always an eternal ember
inside each other's keep

with memories past
going to and paths from
still setting rooms on fire
with the poetry we've become.

Poet Messiah

You are a Poet Messiah
bleeding hymnals
from the crucible of your pen

for your words,
I'd gladly attend service
I'd drink your ink like holy wine

and I must confess,
I'd damn my soul,
worshiping at the altar of your voice

drink of me, this is my blood
take of me, this is my body

willingly, and more willingly
with every page turn
I become revelations

Life and death are in the power of the tongue,
and those who love it will eat its fruit.[1]

---

[1] Italicized lines: Proverbs 18:21

so, give me every plum of poetry
every ripe cherry of wisdom
written inside your heavenly orchard

maketh me a poem
feasting on Divine light
it is phosphene to my hungry soul.

A Fairytale

I think I pulled you from a fairytale
hopeful days of longing
not for rescue or a prince
but someone to lay truths at my feet

and inside them, I would find
my whole self, a perfect fit, a match
but it's midnight and clock strike
has lifted the veil from my eyes

only the myth of us remains
a glamour spell
evanescent as a scent
dissipating with time

eating everything
it crackles the wick
struggling for a flame
snuffed by drowning wax

until hamster wheels
reveal what is real,
and the dream curls backward
like paper from a book

into shadow, our pretenses fall
who we pretended we were
and the truth is, I don't know
because the ending lacked morals.

The Prospect of Dying

Does the leaf fear its fall
dread its moldering decay or
cry for its last drop of color, *no*

when I say *grow old with me,*
I am saying, we are the slow song
of dying things reborn to stars

longing for endless dreams Winter brings,
and the secret lullabies Summer reveals
inside Spring's awakening cradle.

Photograph

Is it possible to know you
through a photograph
to trade some element
of existential loneliness
I perceive, for the I am
I long to be or
who I imagine
you are or
we could be
inside this 2D
black-and-white world

still, it is only a piece
a once but forever fragment
where I can keep you
and love you in a paradox
of perceived love—
you, beyond the lens
me, behind the lens
beautiful and perfect
and us, perfect within
the captured narrative.

Black Pearls

We thought we were invisible
two grains of sand
under streetlights
haloed in summer humidity

but our shadows scraped
and our ears grated
against the loud silence
we fought to escape

inside whisky delirium
channeling restless blood
we forged selfish poetry
inked with poisoned pens

became invincible together
against pending storms
until inhibitions pried open and
glass mouths drowned us

until scars of truths
buoyed the surface
exposing years of illusions
no longer filling the abyss

we weren't right
but we weren't wrong
we were forging black pearls
in shells of mourning.

Thistle Fox

I once believed
I wasn't deserving of love—

an encumbering thing
a destination ending in pain

and so, I practiced being solivagant
I became a thistle

in a field of bramble
I cinctured my color

against poetic ardors
I barbed needed touches

but then I saw you
bramble fox

red and full of fire
aethereal footed

despite the cuts
you brought me a snail

laid it before my feet
as if to say, *I will wait for you*

then you prayed to my colors
until your eyes turned lavender

and you licked my barbs
with a bloody tongue

and burned the bramble
into bliss and said,

now there is only us
and I believed you.

Reincarnation

If I experience life again,
may I embody his soul

feel his love for her
as ancient as a myth

give me his eyes
their hazel swell

his skin's earthy smell
his touch of her for the first time

may I see her as he did
not through muddy lens

but as a sacred thing
calling him to worship

may I be the growl
behind his voice

the sting to his sex
inviting her to his desire

may I find the green girl
the me, I couldn't see

who tamed his tempest
every time she said, I love you.

Still

And sometimes,
I am still a little girl
in a cardboard box
covered in mudpie offerings

I am still full of acorn pockets
and Autumn's fire
still writing poetry in the sand
when I know I am a shell

I still think about the one I broke
saying *it's only a shell*
knowing it was much more
but too young to understand

that everything is a poem
was once a poem
and everything will be
a poem

and sometimes I forget
what I wish I could remember
and remember what
I wish I could forget

and so, I kiss the petal
knowing it will die
and embrace the nettle
because it longs to be soft

I collect the shells
but only the broken ones
because they, too,
wish to be whole

and I still offer
mudpie confessions
to the storm clouds
that wash me clean

and blow kisses
to animals in the sky
who remember me
and want to play

and still, I burn for everything
the way the sun burns for the moon
who smiles at the girl
in the cardboard box.

Maps

I read your words
and knew you'd read mine

dissolving distance
turning ink into a mirror

I traveled
on bookmarked wings

to page 151
and saw myself

for the first time
not lost

nor a wanderer
but a destination

a full stop
in your poem.

A Library of Friends

Inspired by *How Should One Read a Book?* by Virginia Woolf

Look how they gather
in a room of their own
some old, some juvenile
defined by their stories

journeys, heartbreak, and intrigue
though, I scan from left to right
I'm unsure which one I want
who will keep me company

I cannot judge them by their faces
only the content of their characters,
which are mysterious
and certain to speak volumes

some, I must confess
are terrible bores, dry as bones
others bend and break me
intoxicate and stir my senses

until their black and white pearls
reveal truths as revelations
and I, in my drunken solitude,
find they have chosen me.

Last Call

Loss ticks like a slow 8th metronome
sticky thick in its grieving pace
everything feels like your departure
like amber drink evaporating
in a shrinking glass

so, I drink slowly
hoping to control time
knowing Time controls me
knowing nothing changes the wait
or weight of when I will see you again.

Diagnosis Aftermath

I’ve not been a good mother
despite what you say
some things still overshadow
all I’ve done right

I will always blame myself
for your diagnosis and mine
I am too full of doubtful possibility
I will always have questions

was it the postpartum depression or
choosing not to breastfeed you
was I too cold, distant, and selfish
was I never meant to be a mother

was it the sips of wine I had
at eight months pregnant, or the bottles
I consumed after your birth
I’ll play those skipped records forever

all the things I should have done
shouldn’t have done
should have said
shouldn’t have said

the imprints
I spilled on your threshold
the insecurities
I tattooed under your skin

my emptiness
invading your atoms
my scars
clipping your wings

mothers are not perfect
even though you say I am
I will always wonder if
I loved you enough.

Beneath the Blue

Cloud faces envelope the sky
I wonder what is beyond the blue
stars, nebula, God—
nothing

I want to fly, but am afraid, and so,
I kiss the ground with curling toes and
smell the earth's breath exhale
the sweetness of her turning

I think everything is theater
a backdrop to being
a film my blood writes
and bones wish to live

everything is drifting
between life and loss
while the middle swarms
with plot possibilities

what could be
what I wish to be
what I will never become
and underneath it all,

I wonder if the script is real
if an epiphany is a lie, and
I am just an actor on a stage
pretending to tell the truth.

Glamour Fades

I romanticized you
lost myself in the glamour
behind your eyes

forests of burnt acorns
endless embers of twilight
and dreams of faerie darkness

oh, how I was captivated
pixie-led by your reaping Soul
feasting at your table

begging to please you
be a feather in your wing
too foolish to see the harm

but you were a dash of light
and I was a gypsy moth
drawn to false light enchantment

ensnared in the entropy
believing your dominion
was my salvation

when you were only an illusion,
and I was temporary—
we were dewdrops on a thorn.

The House That Love Built

A golden shovel, from a line in Laurie Lee's "Moss-Rose"

We are endless. And from our graves, Time will draw
upon our decaying bones. And from them,
feed life into the dying muse. And from moss, shape
seeds into flowers. And form words from
a million atoms, restless with the
need to release every joy and thorn
hidden within shadowed soil. New shoots will lay
our stories over naked ground, and from them
become gardens of roses. Or perhaps, we will be like
the fathomless abyss or salt to the bleeding
sea. Upon its frothing shore, we will rest our shells,
neith the moon to become the poetry Poets dream about
writing. When nothing is left but the ethereal, the
myth of us will linger forever in Love's eternal house.

I'll Be in Paris

lost in discursive thoughts
wandering Pere Lachaise
searching for Jim, Oscar,
and Marcel Marceau

afterward, I'm off to find
the perfect book and croissant,
or crack a Crème Brule in
a quaint Parisian café

next up, the Eiffel Tower
a stroll down the Champs-Élysées
like Alice in Wonderland
I'll rabbit hop the day away

words can wait in lonely lists
future days of creation
eyeing me in hopeful anticipation
like tourists at a train station

without a map or a destination
lost in translation, blocked
from spaces becoming Pinterest
pages of procrastination.

Time
clears lens
of yesterday's fog
exposing hidden epiphanies of
truth.

About the Author

Trisha Leigh Shufelt is an award-winning poet, self-taught mixed media artist, and breast cancer survivor. Trisha's work leans toward confessional poetry with an emphasis on nature. She often draws upon her own experience with addiction, anxiety, and loss. She is the author of several poetry books, including *The Ghosts of Nevermore,* winner of a 2023 Saturday Visiter Award from the Edgar Allan Poe House and Museum in Baltimore, MD. Her work has also appeared in several poetry anthologies. She edited *Passion for Poetry,* a poetry review journal for poets and poetry lovers.

You can find out more about Trisha at:
www.trishaleighpoetry.com

www.ingramcontent.com/pod-product-compliance
Lightning Source LLC
LaVergne TN
LVHW090535110826
845146LV00003B/1113

* 9 7 9 8 9 0 1 4 6 7 2 8 2 *